G.R.A.B. Tomorrow:

Your Best Year Ever

By Mike Abramowitz

Published by Mike Abramowitz

11380 66th Street #134, Largo, FL 33773

© G.R.A.B. TOMORROW 2015

Terms and Conditions:

.

Everything I am or ever hope to be,
I owe to my angel mother

A portion of the purchase price of this book will be donated to "PB&J for USA." in effort to feed 600,000 homeless people each year across the nation. We recognize that those who find themselves upon hard times should never be overlooked. Life is unpredictable and at any moment the tragedy of an unforeseen circumstance could leave even the most stable person in a similar situation. Our hearts reach out and remind those people that they DO matter and that there are still people who care. Everyone deserves to eat.

For information on how you can support "PB&J for USA" please find us on Facebook or visit www.GRABtomorrow.org

"IF I CHANGE, EVERYTHING CHANGES."

- JIM ROHN

CONTENTS

Note from Mike   10

Foreword by JV Crum III   14

Preface   16

Chapter 1: Your Pattern of Behavior   18

Chapter 2: Control Your Thoughts, Control Your Life   24

Chapter 3: Creating Your Change NOW!   46

Chapter 4: Your Best Year Starts NOW!   54

Conclusion: My Call To Action For You   59

Acknowledgments   62

Next Action Steps   65

What is G.R.A.B. Tomorrow?   69

About the Author   72

Note from Mike:

Welcome! I am thrilled that you are taking the initiative to read this book. I was in college when I read a book that changed my life. Immediately after completing that book, I took massive action and bought my first home at the age of twenty. That book was the #1 New York Times bestseller at the time; it's been on the bestseller list since 1997, when it was released; it's now rated as the #1 personal finance book of all time. It's called *Rich Dad, Poor Dad* and dramatically changed my life and my thoughts about utilizing my resources. My goal is to create a shift in your perspective that will allow you to take massive action towards your goals upon completing this book.

G.R.A.B. Tomorrow started as an idea geared toward helping young professionals gain control of their lives outside of the classroom. Just a month later, we launched a website (www.GRABtomorrow.org), a Facebook page with one thousand supporters at the time of this book release, and this book, which starts the G.R.A.B. Tomorrow series. This series includes books, journals, planners, virtual workshops, coaching, and live events. We also began a sub-series of books called "Real Stories, Real People" that are filled with stories of individuals living their lives using the G.R.A.B. philosophies. These stories are uplifting, inspiring, and really capture the reader's attention. The goal of this community as a whole is to influence people – and in particular students and young professionals – to follow their desires outside of the classroom, regardless of their circumstances or conditions.

In 2012, job placement firm Adecco stated that 60% of U.S. college graduates could not find a job in their chosen profession. The Accenture 2014 College Graduate Employment Survey result show that only 48% of college graduates receive training from their first employer, 41% are earning $25,000 or less, and 42% are living at home with parents. According to the National Postsecondary Student Aid Study (NPSAS), 71% of all students graduating from four-year colleges have student loan debt. That equals 1.3 million students with an average debt of $29,000. Would it not make sense to help students avoid these trends and provide them with tools that will allow them to create a path with more training, more income, and more control over their futures?

Regardless of their socio-economic conditions and statistical trends, they can still thrive in a world where odds tend to be against them before they even enter it. The G.R.A.B. community is designed to guide students through a simple, yet effective path that will lead them towards a life where they can create options. Options instill control and confidence. Options allow students to have a feeling of certainty.

I am certain that the tools provided in the G.R.A.B. Tomorrow series will equip tomorrow's leaders with the know-how to create the life that their potential offers.

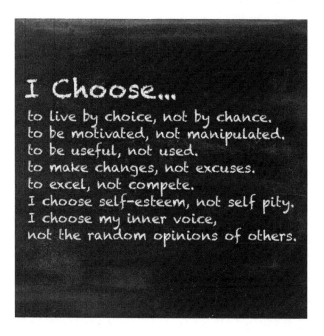

I Choose...
to live by choice, not by chance.
to be motivated, not manipulated.
to be useful, not used.
to make changes, not excuses.
to excel, not compete.
I choose self-esteem, not self pity.
I choose my inner voice,
not the random opinions of others.

Say YES
to your life

Foreword by J V Crum III:

What if today could be the turning point in your life? What if this could be the year that you got clear about what it means for you to live your dream? What if you then took the specific steps necessary to turn your dream life into your new, exciting reality?

Further, what if you had a step-by-step guidebook that would teach, guide, and help ensure that you would GRAB Your Tomorrow and create the destiny that you so desire?

My friend, Mike Abramowitz, has created such a guidebook. In *G.R.A.B. Tomorrow: Your Best Year Ever*, Mike takes you on a journey of awakening: first, to what is actually possible for your life and second, on how you, too, can now achieve it.

Isn't it time that you took control over your life and destiny?

If you are like more than 90% of young professionals, then you probably aren't sure about what is actually possible for your life. You may not have precise goals for your next year or a plan for how you will absolutely, with complete certainty, attain them.

Just reading "absolutely, with complete certainty" probably brought up some fear and anxiety in you.

That's understandable. Few young professionals ever achieve the amazing life that Mike is going to ask you to achieve. They never do more than scratch the surface of what is possible for their lives during their twenties. Even fewer ever test their limits or dare to attempt to live up to their dreams.

The truth: most young professionals don't take control of their life; don't develop real confidence; don't create clear and challenging goals; don't design a realistic plan for achieving their goals; and, as a result, fail to tap into and use all their potential.

What is the result? They simply fail to build the life of their dreams, in every respect – personally, in their relationships, in their careers, and in their finances.

But that doesn't have to be you. Unlike the majority of your peers, those people who resign themselves to a life of abject mediocrity, you can now make another choice. You can consciously choose to make this the year in which you don't just dream, but you actually learn how to excel at your highest levels!

Mike Abramowitz can be your trusted guide. He is one of the millennial visionaries, and utilized both his own personal experience and the knowledge gained by coaching and training thousands of college students and young professionals, to write *G.R.A.B. Tomorrow: Your Best Year Ever*.

Complete with exercises and worksheets, Mike's book contains the information you need in order to go from wherever you are at this moment to living the life of your dreams – this year!

You can make a decision, right now, this moment, that this will be the year in which you will stop dreaming and hoping and instead will commit to getting it all: life your way, on your terms.

J V Crum III, JD, MBA, MS Psy

Founder, ConsciousMillionaire.com

Host, http://www.ConsciousMillioanirePodcast.com

Author: "Conscious Millionaire: Grow Your Business by Making a Difference"

Preface:

There have been times in everyone's life where we've wanted to accomplish things and then, for any number of reasons, simply allowed our goals to fall by the wayside. *G.R.A.B. Tomorrow: Your Best Year Ever* is designed to challenge you on exactly this point: it will help you master the skill of commitment, of follow-through, of getting things done. Half of the battle is showing up and implementing the knowledge that you already have. By taking the step to read this book, it shows that you are ready to leave the past behind and "G.R.A.B" the future you desire.

It's normal to fall prey to distractions. We fill our schedules up with items that don't move us closer to the life we desire. We start to just let life happen, instead of pursuing a life that we are truly excited about.

I learned in my early twenties the power of having a vision and a strategic plan. Those two tools can create an intrinsic shift when executed correctly. Think about some of the most influential figures in history: Walt Disney, Thomas Edison, Michael Jordan, Martin Luther King Jr., Oprah Winfrey… They are or were all visionaries. They were able to see the future far beyond the circumstances they were living in. Having vision is being able to see the invisible. It is about being able to look beyond where we have been and into where we are going.

Your past results are consequences of previous decisions, actions, and attitudes. By dwelling on the past, we will continue to get the same results. We must take those experiences as simple lessons we can learn from. By taking a step back and analyzing where we have been, we can find a way of facing challenges more effectively in the future. We can become solution finders.

The premise of *G.R.A.B. Tomorrow: Your Best Year Ever* is to help you get through personal struggles in a less time consuming, more productive way. When you follow the guidelines in this book, you will reach a potential that might have been unreachable last year.

Just reading this book, however, is not the secret you're doubtlessly looking for. You will enjoy the information and it will be useful to you. If you want to get outstanding results and really have the best year of your life, I am going to encourage you to step over the edge. I want you to succeed at unimaginable levels.

The time spent reading this book, however, is not what will create the outcome. It will be your commitment to taking massive action. It is crucial, then, to do the exercises when you get to them. These are critical to building momentum throughout the book and to training your subconscious mind to think in a way that will serve you best. This will be the first step towards creating "your best year ever".

So, before you read any further, grab a pen or pencil. As you progress, there will be exercises that you'll need to fill out in order to make the most out of this book. Its purpose is not to remain untouched, but rather to offer you all the value you can extract from it. So you have my permission... mark this book up!

I encourage you to follow every step and to write down the answers to the questions during the "Exercise to Thrive". This journey will *only* be effective and create results when you risk vulnerability and take your "Exercise to Thrive" seriously.

I remember attending my first dance lesson at the 1st Dance Studio in Saint Petersburg, Florida, back in 2013. I was extremely nervous to attend; I didn't know anyone at the dance studio and had never attended a lesson before. I didn't know what to expect. I had to risk feeling vulnerable and experience the discomfort, if I wanted to improve my dancing skills. I had to risk not knowing the outcome.

After my first year, I completed my first competition, made many new friends, and surprised myself with how much improvement I made overall. Throughout the process of learning how to dance, I kept a journal about my experience. I documented some uncomfortable moments and exciting ones. My journal captured these moments as if it were a photo album. When I review some of my dancing experiences, it reminds me of how much progress I made.

By documenting your thoughts throughout this book, you will be able to re-visit them at a later time as though it were a photo album of your own. Without documentation, your experiences will be lost. Think about how often we take a look at a photo and say, "I forgot about that!" According to the National Science Foundation, we have over 50,000 thoughts that go through our minds daily. It is time to take control of these thoughts, separate yourself from who you were, and start making room for who you are becoming.

This is a courageous move and I am excited to guide you through to "your best year ever!" It is time to ROCK your year!

Chapter 1
Your Pattern of Behavior

What is S.A.M.?
How do I create better results in my personal and professional life THIS year?

When I was growing up in New Jersey as the youngest of eight children, I was different from my siblings in one aspect: they, unlike me, were all average or above average when it came to their physical health. My dad had a pretty big influence on them because he'd been a bodybuilder growing up. At nineteen years old, he won the Mr. Trenton bodybuilding tournament without any steroids or enhancers, and this was only one of many competitions he won throughout the next decade. My three older brothers followed in his footsteps and were bodybuilders and obsessed with being fit.

We had trophies around the back room of our house to honor their achievements. My oldest sister was into yoga and my oldest brother was into rowing and running. My other two sisters were skinny and average-sized, and I? I was struggling at seventy pounds overweight going into high school.

My dad would bribe me to lose weight; at one point, he offered me $5 per pound that I lost in a one-week time frame. I remember feeling so down about my physical condition that I would end up eating *more* to offset my pain. The situation was such that I'd sneak Twinkies into my bedroom. I was sneaking these treats into my room so the others wouldn't find out, but in retrospect, who was I really hurting?

It seemed unreachable for me to lose weight during my adolescence. Eventually, I simply accepted my situation – because it was easier to accept than it was to change. I would just eat through my internal conflict about my health. I'd act as if I didn't care, but internally, I was crying for help. I lacked an immense amount of confidence. I was bullied in school and would fight to prove that I was tough like my older siblings, but I felt really weak on the inside. In my early teens, I was overly emotional, I lacked self-control, and I gave excuses as to why I couldn't get fit and accepted my life of being overweight. What did all that help me with? Not much!

I've realized that *easy* is not what we need in life. We need obstacles and challenges in order to grow. When we are growing, we are living. People are just like bananas: we are either growing up or growing rotten; there is no in-between. And often when faced with big challenges, we *know* what to do, but we still don't do it. The challenge itself is simply too daunting to face head-on!

So we must make the challenge simpler. We must break it down into smaller obstacles that we can see ourselves accomplishing, and then grow through them. We must take daily action steps. This is why SAM is so effective. SAM is a pattern of behavior. When SAM is followed, you will:

- be in control of your life
- increase your confidence
- have a plan of daily steps to follow towards achieving your goals
- have clarity on what you want and which traps to avoid
- strengthen relationships that are important to you
- start living the life you deserve to live

SAM is an acronym, which stands for:
S - Strategy – a careful plan or method for achieving a goal
A - Action – the process of doing something
M - Mindset – the established set of attitudes held by someone

SAM is a leadership tool that helps you focus and strengthen yourself. The skills you need to change your community and your own mindset for the better are learnable through SAM. It is one of the pillars of the G.R.A.B. Tomorrow community, which is dedicated to fostering confident, change-driven, and inspiring leaders.

A leader with a powerful conviction garners loyalty, support, and instills principles in those who follow them. They create massive change this way: by teaching others to be compassionate, to strive for change as they do, and by influencing their supporters to takes a stand for what they believe in. Amazing leaders like Oprah Winfrey, Steve Jobs, Rosa Parks, Henry Ford, and many more have all created massive social movements.

Leaders of this caliber create change in our communities because a person with an inspiring vision, as evidenced by the achievements of these giants, has the capacity to change the course of history. Think about the abolishment of slavery; the civil rights movement; the way the very concepts of humanitarianism and the role of a First Lady were redefined; the theory of Relativity – the achievements of Abraham Lincoln, Martin Luther King Jr., Mother Teresa, Eleanor Roosevelt, and Albert Einstein, respectively. Future leaders are able to look back on history and see that these giants all desired a brighter future.

The G.R.A.B. Tomorrow community is dedicated to influencing aspiring leaders to think about life outside of the classroom this way, and to create desired change that will make their community a better place to live. Toward that end, SAM is a very important tool.

In order for SAM to create desired results, we must make sure that we have the right focus. Think of something simple: taking an important exam at school and being distracted by all the other things that are happening in your life that do not have to do with the test. No matter how many notes are written on your note card or cheat sheet, by not being present, we won't get the desired results. We will start with two exercises that will get us focused and make sure we are present:

Exercise to Thrive One: "Attitude of Gratitude"

I want you to take a moment prior to continuing and write down as fast as you can everything you have in your life that you are grateful for. I want you to consider the following Ps: People, Places, Possessions, and Privileges. Consider also some of the principles you live your life by, and what positive impacts they've had on you.

What are you grateful for right now?

_____
_____
_____
_____
_____

Beginning the day or any activity with gratitude is like walking into a room and turning on the lights. All you do is flip the switch and enjoy the benefits that the light brings you. When you begin by writing down a list of all the things that you are grateful for, it allows you a sense of perspective. These are the important things in your life, and remembering them makes you more present in your day.

It takes courage to be grateful in a cynical society. It doesn't take any courage to be negative. The cliché is "life sucks" – and the people who adhere to it might believe that their life does indeed "suck", but in most cases, I've found that these people are simply gutless. They are not willing to risk the vulnerability that being positive brings. That wall that protects us from being grateful and appreciating the things we have in our lives also separates us from being in our best state of mind to really capture the potential that we are all capable of tapping into.

I have found that when I'm grateful, I'm present with my priorities, which makes me rich. Money is not the key to being rich, gratitude is. I am filled with joy that you are taking the time to really appreciate everything that you have and reminding yourself of all the benefits that will come from it – memories, relationships, lessons, a good attitude. By reflecting on all of the things we have, feeling grateful for them, and intentionally creating our mood, we are allowing ourselves to be present and ready to take action.

Exercise to Thrive Two: "What's HOT?"

I want you to take a moment prior to continuing and write down as fast as you can everything that is happening in your life that you are excited about, proud of, or working towards personally and professionally.

Example: I am most proud of reading one book per month right now **OR** *I am working towards bettering the relationship with my sister intentionally.*

_____
_____
_____
_____
_____
_____
_____
_____
_____

Have you ever had to do something but not felt like doing it? It happens to me all the time. How do I still take action? Well, I remind myself of the progress that I made previously. By reviewing my progress, I realize that I am moving in the right direction: towards my goals.

The moments that I get caught in a routine without a reminder of my progress are the moments that I become discouraged, especially if the rewards I reap aren't what I expected. Anytime our experiences do not match our expectations, there will be internal conflict. The goal is to tie our emotions and expectations to the *process*, not the *reward*. The emotion that the reward brings only lasts for a limited period of time. The emotion that *progress* brings can be transferred to any other facet of your life.

For example, when I complete a book, it gives me an immediate and very specific sense of accomplishment, like checking an item off of a to-do list. In this scenario, I focus only on the end result. But the process is more important: when I teach someone a concept from a book that I am currently reading, it's because I am learning from it and using that knowledge to serve others, which makes we want to continue to read and learn and teach.

Now, imagine being in a relationship and never celebrating the milestones, anniversaries, and emotional progress that you are making as a couple. The relationship milestones are a way of evaluating yourselves; of celebrating how you've grown and surpassed obstacles. They move us forward consistently, and that forward momentum will eventually lead us to our goals.

The next few chapters will include many great clarifying questions and exercises that will allow you to unlock ideas, dreams, goals, aspirations, desires, and everything in between. I am honored to have the opportunity to take you on this journey to "your best year ever" and grateful to show you some amazing results THIS year!

We will begin with mindset: helping you think the right way. Then we will discuss some strategies and steps to take towards your goals. We will then go through some simple action steps to commit to in order to maintain the process of growth towards your goals. Get ready! It's time to G.R.A.B. your best year ever!

Notes Page

Chapter 2
Control Your Thoughts, Control Your Life

Mindset Development
"Move Past Your Past"

Growing up as the youngest of eight children in NJ, I was always viewed as "the baby" of the family. No matter how old I got, I was still the baby, and considered a huge "mama's boy" because I had the mindset that no matter what happened in life, my mother would always be there to save me. And she always was. I have a lifetime of stories that prove that, but if I had to pick one, I'd pick this little one:

There was a storm coming through our hometown and my friends and I were thirteen years old and stranded at the bowling alley. This was before everyone had cell phones. There was a tornado warning, so we were nervous to walk home. Within five minutes of  leaving the bowling alley, a car pulls up and my mom rolls down her window and says, "Do you boys need a ride home? I was just in the neighborhood!" We all piled in her car and were rescued from the storm. She was always there to save me growing up, which made me extremely reliant on her, both emotionally and for everyday things.

When I graduated high school, I decided to move away from my hometown and attend college at the University of South Florida, in Tampa. Two years prior to this decision, my mom was diagnosed with ovarian cancer. At that point in time, she was given six months to live. I was sixteen years old and didn't quite grasp the severity of the situation.

"Yeah, right! Six months! She's unstoppable! It's mom! She'll be fine!" As a naïve junior in high school, I thought there was no way anything could ever happen to my mom. She ended up undergoing an operation that removed a tumor the size of a grapefruit from her ovary and went into remission. Throughout all of this, it was decided that we wouldn't communicate the six-month prognosis to her. Even though *she* didn't know about it, I knew my mom was a fighter and that she was too strong to allow words like "six months" to get in her way.

I think my mom was able to make it through that six-month period because her mindset was "I'll be fine. I got this." She never thought about anything different than beating this disease and making it through to whatever was next in life. From my mom, I learned that anything our mind is convinced of is our reality. We've all heard the saying "mind over matter". If the mind believes something to be true, it is. If my mom believed six months was all she had, as the doctors did, who knows what would have happened. But she believed that this disease was a short-term battle, and she was home a few weeks later.

My decision to leave home knowing that my mom was battling cancer was challenging. My mom was able to make the decision much easier for me. She said, "Michael, I love you and I want you to stay here with me, but I know you're meant for great things. Florida seems like it'll be the place to make those things happen for you. You're only a plane ride away from home, so you'll visit, right? If you don't, I'll get the room next to yours!"

My mom was right; Florida did have a good life waiting for me and she was only a flight away. I made my journey to Florida in my red 1991 Mitsubishi Eclipse, which was a hand-me-down from my sister-in-law. I was so ready for my independence. No more nagging about doing the dishes, taking out the trash, cleaning my room, or staying out late. I was free!

And yet, after unpacking, I immediately felt homesick. I realized very quickly that a lot of independence meant equal levels of responsibility, and that simple shift in perspective created a lot of pressure. It got real for me. I was finally at a point in my life where I was in control; it was time to be a man.

My mom was in remission for a few years. I confidently enjoyed my first year of college and visited home only for the holidays. But that peaceful time was limited. At the start of my sophomore year of college, I received a phone call: the cancer had returned aggressively. Mom returned to the hospital with only "a week to live" this time.

As my mom and I agreed, I was only a plane ride away from home, right? So my mindset was to handle everything! I balanced my sales position with Vector Marketing, five engineering classes, my responsibilities as a manger in the office, and also my life skills development program for an internship that the company had lined up for me the following summer.

I fit everything into five days and then caught the 9PM flight to

Newark each Friday night. Most of the time, I took the midnight train to the hospital and slept on an air mattress on the floor. Sometimes, my friends at Rutgers would pick me up from the airport and let me crash on their couches. I spent time with my mom and my family for the weekend. We loved watching Disney movies, Family Feud, and an occasional Miami Dolphins football game. We went through photo albums and home videos and talked about all of the funny stories and memories we shared. We laughed. We cried. We enjoyed being a family, regardless of the circumstances.

BE BOLD
BE COURAGEOUS
BE YOUR BEST

I would then catch the 5PM flight back to Tampa on Sunday and begin my week all over again. I did this twenty-six times throughout an eight-month period. So much for one week to live! The strength my mom demonstrated proves to me that anything is possible.

My mindset throughout this process was to take one week at a time and be present with whatever was in front of me. When I was in school, I focused on school. When I was with a client, I focused on my client. When I was with my mom, I was present with my mom.

Of course, as a twenty year old, this was challenging; I was witnessing my mother and best friend battling this aggressive disease taking over her body. I had many breakdowns and oftentimes considered dropping out of college; just returning home to be with family, and then continuing my education later in life. My circle of influence, however, kept reminding me of how capable I was and urging me to keep moving forward. One of my mentors would say, "Stay focused, stay present, and keep pushing through."

I now realize how valuable that advice would be throughout my twenties. I used that advice when the market collapsed and I lost my life savings as well as the properties that I had invested in. I used that advice when my best friend and college roommate was in a fatal car accident. I used that advice when my girlfriend of seven years and I decided to end our relationship. I used that advice throughout my ten years of selling Cutco as a student entrepreneur.

Many lessons about mindset came to me during this time frame:

- do not listen to other people's opinions when they don't serve to make me better
- be present with what is in front of me
- it's okay to ask for help
- surround myself with people who care, that will challenge and support me
- anything is possible with enough intentional focus

These are lessons that are easily replicated and I will show you how to implement them.

The first lesson about mindset that can be easily learned is this: always make sure to remind yourself of your own potential. When we are at our best, we feel unstoppable! When we are fully present and feeling confident, our goals don't stand a chance of not getting accomplished.

Think about a time when you had to get in the zone and act your best in order to make a great first impression. Maybe it was for a job interview or meeting a significant other's parents for the first time. For me, it was the time I tried out for the eighth grade basketball team.

Tryouts were a nightmare for me, particularly because I didn't want to associate with the other kids who were trying out. I'd gotten into fistfights with them all through seventh grade just so they'd get off my case. I was the pimple kid: freckles, braces, glasses, overweight, but I had heart. I had determination. So I tried out for the basketball team.

I'd never tried out for a sport. I almost didn't, just because I thought I wouldn't make it. During the exercises, I was last place every time – but I ran and I ran, until I ended up with a cramp in my side.

The coach pulled me aside at the end of the try-outs.

He sat me on a bench and said, "Mike, your attitude and your work ethic is unmatchable and I need a guy like you on my team."

And I said, "Sir, are you sure? Did you – you saw what just happened, right? I was last place every time, right?"

And he said, "Heart like that is hard to find."

A tool to help us remember what our best looks like is journaling. The act of writing our thoughts down transfers them from the emotional part of our brain to the logical part. Without getting too scientific, journaling allows us to get out of our selves for a moment; it allows us to gain clarity. Through journaling, I have been able to capture snapshots of who I am, who I was, and who I want to be. This has allowed me to start closing the gap between these stages and start unlocking my true potential. Journaling captured my daily progress towards fulfillment and has made a huge impact on my life.

By journaling using some simple questions as your guide, you will start to connect with the best version of yourself – and thus start performing at your highest levels. This leads into the next exercise:

Exercise to Thrive Three: When I am at my best, I...

I want you to think about what it would take to consistently feel good and be at your best. Think about all the moments you had in your life where you felt unstoppable; moments when you expected and demanded a lot from yourself. Moments when you expected less out of the outcome because you knew deep down that the result didn't matter, as long as you just did your best work. Think about your posture, your thoughts, your relationships, your tone of voice, how you treated others, and how you treated and viewed yourself.

Example: When I am at my best, I eat greens, drink water, give compliments, write thank you cards, hold doors for strangers, stand straight, smile, journal daily, read daily.

_____

_____

_____

_____

_____

_____

Since creating this list, I often look back at it as a reminder of who I choose to be. I add to this list throughout the year in order to take better control of my mindset. Our mindset comes from what we tell ourselves repeatedly, and so I continue to remind myself about how I am at my best, which makes me want to continue being that version of myself.

According to the National Science Foundation, 97% of what controls our thoughts is the past. This can, against all odds, be turned into great news, because we can choose which parts of our history we want to focus on. We can focus on our painful past that held us back from our potential, or we can focus on what life is like when we are at our best and the results that follow.

Often times, however, we get caught in the trap of reflecting on things that are not in our control. We think about the news, our past mistakes, our history, the color of our skin, the family we were raised by, the side of town we grew up in, and we focus our energy on things that are not in our control. Think about how limiting that mindset is from a logical standpoint. By investing energy towards something that *cannot be changed*, we are setting ourselves up for failure. In these moments we must use the "5-Minute Rule" and rise above the circumstances.

The "5-Minute Rule" is a concept that was taught to me as a student, to support me in accepting outcomes that were out of my control. Every time there was a situation I faced – a bad appointment with a client or a low test grade or even a traffic ticket – I had five minutes to accept the result and take action towards creating something new. This worked very well for me, because the words "I can't change it" triggered the logical part of my brain. By saying those words, I could simply accept the outcome and move on.

When we approach a situation that we *do* have control over, but never work to solve, the price we pay for our inaction is never moving forward. Staying still is never a viable option towards success. So if we have the ability to overcome a challenge, let's *take action*.

For example, when a student avoids a difficult subject or procrastinates until the last night an assignment is due, they are faced with a challenge that could have been dodged with better habits and planning. The short-term consequence will be a tired and grumpy person who pulled an all-nighter; however, long-term, this student might get stuck in a failing cycle. It's impossible to sustain success outside of the classroom with the habits of procrastination and poor planning because it will eventually begin affecting relationships, work, health, personal endeavors, and diverting energy towards other goals that might seem more appealing because they are easier to obtain. Eventually, this system of procrastination and poor planning will become increasingly detrimental, and a change must take place. Decision-making and planning are both within this student's control.

In my early teens, I mentioned that I was overweight and felt like a victim. I felt like the odds were against me and that I had no control. I felt like overeating and getting bullied were going to be a part of my life forever, so I just had to accept it. Thankfully, a breakthrough finally took place during my transition from eighth grade to high school.

I always had a passion for basketball and grew up as a giant Michael Jordan fan. I watched all of his videos on VHS (some of you might remember those!). I was inspired by his story of being cut from his basketball team in high school and choosing to work really hard to make the team the following year; when his father was killed and he still found a way to honor his dad by pursuing baseball, even though he wasn't very good at it. His actions during circumstances that were out of his control inspired me to try out for the basketball team. I knew I wasn't the most talented eighth grader, nor the most athletic. I needed to take control of myself and just do it!

By making the eighth grade basketball team, I realized that there were strengths that I possessed and that I needed to use them to my advantage. I was an Honor Roll student because of my discipline towards my study habits. In eighth grade, I transferred that same discipline towards getting into better physical shape. I was eager to help the coach and others on the team when they needed assistance. I realized I was a great helper and supporter, and that I needed to offer myself the same encouragement I offered my teammates. I changed the way my inner voice spoke. Instead of saying "you can't" or "you're not good enough", I started saying "you've got this" and "keep pushing". Realizing the control I had over myself was the huge breakthrough I needed in order to shift my focus from being doubtful to being able to take action towards what I truly desired.

THREE SIMPLE RULES IN LIFE

1. IF YOU DO NOT GO AFTER WHAT YOU WANT, YOU'LL NEVER HAVE IT.

2. IF YOU DO NOT ASK, THE ANSWER WILL ALWAYS BE NO.

3. IF YOU DO NOT STEP FORWARD, YOU WILL ALWAYS BE IN THE SAME PLACE.

Often times, we need an event to trigger a shift in our mindset. So often we get too caught up in our daily routine, and neglect to take a moment to think about where we are and where we are going. I was using the 5-Minute Rule throughout my late teens for the smaller-scale items in my life, as I mentioned earlier, but the event that really helped me implement the 5-Minute Rule and take control of my procrastination was when my mom lost the battle to cancer.

Prior to her losing this battle, I was guilty of putting things off until the last minute, as any normal teen does. I would wait until deadlines were given to me, instead of creating my own deadlines. Witnessing my mom's deadline on life was a devastating time, yet it was also an awakening. It forced me to take control of my life, and the things that I desired. I was twenty years old and realizing that my childhood hero and best friend was no longer here – and that the amount of time that I have on this planet is finite. I realized it was time to grow through this event and continue towards my dreams and goals with purpose and intention.

I started to understand the two different types of growth that I would experience throughout life: circumstantial growth and intentional growth. Circumstantial growth is triggered by things that are out of our control, such as the death of a loved one, the culture we're born into, damaging weather events, or even the size of our feet. Intentional growth is self-inflicted growth, such as running a marathon, learning a language, instrument, or sport, public speaking, or embracing a fear.

I learned through my life experiences to utilize intentional growth in order to prepare for the circumstantial growth. Intentional growth is in my control and proves my capacity when life's tests happen. I understood that if I wanted to continue being the best version of myself, I needed to continue reminding myself of the goals I had and of my potential.

One of the many lessons I learned from my mom was to keep fighting for what I want. She fought for years because she knew that none of her children were ready for her to pass away. Instead of giving up and ending the pain she was in, she chose to fight.

She dragged out the dying process for her children, intentionally. She finally gave up the fight when she knew that we were ready. She is a true hero in my eyes and the people she came in contact with. Let's take some lessons from my mother, Eleanor Abramowitz, as we transition into some important questions that are designed to trigger intrinsic motivation.

The following exercises include some questions and tools that will allow you to gain clarity and focus in order to avoid being caught up in the things you cannot control and to influence the things you can.

We will start with BIG thinking! This is one of the most exciting exercises you'll experience. I learned this exercise while I was a student and it helped me gain clarity surrounding what I wanted out of life. At first, it seemed unimaginable to me that I could write down my dreams and actually be intentional about achieving them. I thought that whatever happens in life, happens. This exercise helped me unlock the truth to what I wanted, including a stronger relationship with my dad and sister, traveling to Switzerland, taking a road trip with my niece, writing a book, and many others. Many professional speakers and authors use this tool to help unlock people's true desires. It's called a "Dream-Storming Session" and it's designed to help you figure out what you would want out of life if resources were limitless.

Exercise to Thrive Four: Dream-Storming Session

I want you to think about as many things as possible that you want in life, from each category. Regardless of resources (money, time, energy) and fears (flying, rejection, failure), just dream! You want to take a few seconds for each and not spend too much time over-thinking. Write whatever comes to your head!

Remember, regardless of resources, JUST DREAM! You have an entire lifetime. Could you think of over fifty dreams? Maybe it's one hundred dreams? More? We will see! Enjoy crafting your life!

At least three places to visit anywhere in the world

Changes within your home (kitchen, pool, Jacuzzi, bedroom, etc.)

Changes to the car you drive

Ideal fitness levels

Your target yearly earnings within the next five years

Size of your retirement fund

Which relationships would you like to improve

Learn any languages

Learn to play any instruments

Write a book about these topics

Meet any living person

Meet any person from history

Conquer any fears

What are your business/career dreams?

Connect with someone from your past

What do you want to be remembered for?

Live in any city

Vacation home

If you had $10,000 cash today, what would you buy?

Road trip to where and with whom?

Congrats on your first Dream-Storming Session! As you become more familiar with dreaming big and communicating your goals with other people, you will start adding more to the list. I would challenge you to go back and count them up. See how close you are to one hundred dreams! If you're not there yet, keep at it. Dreams are like a buffet: you can have as much as you want.

I know the first time I did this exercise, I was thinking, "It'd be nice to make some of these happen." According to Matthew Kelly, bestselling author and professional speaker, only 1% of the world actually takes the time to make a list of their goals and only 1% of that 1% will make an action plan to start achieving them. When I heard this, I made a commitment that I would not let my dreams slide. When we gain clarity on what those dreams are, we develop an intrinsic motivation to achieve them; a motivation that allows you to go through the discomfort and embody the eagerness to rise every morning. I consider myself to be in the 1% of those who capture their dreams and I am excited for you to join me!

Exercise to Thrive Five: Dream-Storming Action Plan
From this dreams list, I want you to choose which dreams you can work towards by your birthday, two years from now. This will allow you to start making some of them real. This doesn't mean you absolutely will attain them, it just means you want to make progress towards them within the next two years.

Example:
Dreams list = Play drums in a band
Two years from today list = Begin drum lessons

Personal example:
Dreams list = Own a motorcycle
My 2015 deadline = Have a savings account for a motorcycle

By my birthday, two years from today, I want …

_____

_____

_____

_____

_____

_____

_____

If you have not completed the previous exercises, **PLEASE DO NOT CONTINUE THIS BOOK!** For the remainder of the exercises, you'll need your responses in order to create "your best year ever". This book is designed to help you create the life you desire. Imagine if you could see yourself ten years from now, finding a copy of this book in a box with all of your responses in it: your inner thoughts, your goals, your dreams, your desires. I want you to imagine sitting down next to that box and reading all of your responses with a smile on your face, and counting how many of them came true. Imagine sharing these responses with your kids or loved ones and explaining to them how dreams do come true when you simply write them down. I urge you to not rob yourself of that future moment. Take a few minutes and complete the exercises that may have been skipped. GRAB your pen and make this book come to life!

Let's begin by gaining clarity on what we want this year to be about. Now that you have a list of several dreams you want to get accomplished within the next two years, we must narrow it down to three overall objectives or categories that those dreams can fit into. Some of the students I've completed this exercise with used a few of the following categories: contribution to my community, first-time-ever experiences, saving money, reaching a sales milestone, donating to 100 charities, writing a book, and random acts of kindness.

This intentional focus makes it simple to remember and also allows you to pinpoint the three main priorities you want to work towards in your life. This also brings a singular focus to your goals, who you are, and what you want to be about this year. If you had a commercial advertising yourself and you had to state the three most important priorities in your life deserving of your attention this year, what would they be? What do you want to be about? What do you want to be known for by your peers?

For example: 2015 for me will be the year of health/fitness, professional speaking, and relationship building

Exercise to Thrive Six: The Three Things
Three things that THIS year will be about. Who am I and what do I want to be about? What do I want to be known for THIS year?

THIS year for me will be the year of:

_____

_____

_____

_____

Now you have a clear focus of what you want THIS year to be about. The next time someone asks you what your New Year's Resolutions are, you can confidently tell them! A great response could be "This year will be about _____ and that will allow me to _____ by my birthday in two years, which is getting me closer to my dreams of accomplishing _____ in my life." Think about the power of clarity, intention, and focus behind that statement! You are on your way to creating "your best year ever"!

Now that you have a general idea of what you want this year to be about and what you will stand for, we want to get specific! We will create a list of specific outcomes, habits needed, traps to avoid and how to avoid them, and create a new vantage point on how to set goals and create ways to achieve them.

Prior to developing my depth of knowledge on goal-setting and creating New Year's Resolutions, I'd simply make a statement about what I wanted for the year. The challenge I always faced was that when it got tough, and it always did, I gave up on my goals. The following year would come around and the cycle would repeat itself. In retrospect, if I had followed a system that tracked the progress I was making, I would have developed a higher confidence to continue towards my goals. Progress brings motivation to continue acting. Now that I understand the power of intentionally drawing out my progress from the previous year, I continue to elevate my outcomes and create the life I desire.

Let's take a step back and draw out some of the progress you experienced last year and the success and lessons that came out of it. I believe that when you look back and gain perspective from the past, it creates a more vivid image your future.

Exercise to Thrive Seven: Greatest Successes from last year

Think about all of your greatest successes from last year. All of the accomplishments, awards, partnerships, relationships, progress, etc. that you are proud of and would like to potentially repeat, brag about in the future, or continue this year. In the past, I have had some awful years, but as I searched for the "gifts" within each painful month of that year, I found some amazing wins that I was able to build on. Success can only build on more success. I invite you to go through each month and draw out your successes that way. Go through each activity that you do daily and think about all of the progress you have made in that activity throughout the year. You can also revisit photos or your journal from last year and remind yourself of any successes that might be worth repeating.

My greatest successes from last year are...

_____

_____

_____

_____

_____

_____

_____

_____

_____

_____

_____

_____

_____

_____

_____

_____

_____

_____

Playing sports throughout my teens taught me a valuable lesson: everything happens on purpose; accidents do not exist. All of the habits we learned and developed in practice formed our skills for the game. Any time we won, the coach would draw out the reasons for the victory. When we lost, we would figure out where we didn't perform to our expectations. I learned that I am in control of the victories and losses of my life.

We want to draw out those habits from your successes in order to see which ones can be replicated. We want to figure out what created them. You'll probably notice that the accomplishments worth mentioning probably didn't happen by luck. There were some habits in place in order to make those successes your reality.

Exercise to Thrive Eight: Habits Developed Last Year
We want to figure out what habits were developed last year, so that when continued this year, they could create similar accomplishments. You want to go through each success and find a routine, pattern, behavior, or habit that was in place in order to make that success happen.

For example:
Success – Creating Dream Job Offer
Habits – Resume enhancers, increased communication skills, read books, did mock interviews, etc.

The habits that helped me reach each of my successes from last year are...

_____

_____

_____

_____

_____

_____

_____

If you wait for the perfect conditions you'll never get anything done

We must remember the challenge behind maintaining those habits consistently. And since these habits and accomplishments were executed last year, we know you are capable of them. By executing these habits next year also, you will create a lifestyle change that impacts the rest of your life.

Sometimes we get weak-minded or lack the energy to achieve some of the goals we have. So we need a constant reminder of WHY those habits are important. You may have heard of will power, but this is "WHY-Power". This is the power that is needed to intrinsically create change. "WHY-Power" is crucial when it comes to being held accountable to following a routine. "WHY-Power" reminds you of the benefits of the work. When you feel good, see progress, and are being reminded constantly of what you will continue to gain from your routine, you will be more likely to sustain it.

Exercise to Thrive Nine: Continue the Habits from Last Year

By continuing these habits, you will continue to see progress in your life. Progress is what will bring you a true sense of accomplishment and happiness. We MUST capture those feelings and remind ourselves of why they are important. Let's capture those emotions in this next exercise and find your "WHY-Power."

For example: By continuing to read one self help book monthly, I will read twelve books that will help me develop myself further this year, which will bring me more knowledge and perspective on how to grow into a better version of myself and influence others to do the same.

By continuing to do _____ this year, it will bring me...

_____

_____

_____

_____

_____

_____

So, we now have the successes from last year, what created those successes, and the feelings that they brought you. When completing this exercise, most people experience one of two emotions:

1. I am a ROCK STAR and I had a great year!
> OR
2. I am disappointed with myself. All I kept thinking about was how I didn't follow through on my goals and aspirations.

Both are natural experiences. The first time I did these exercises, my feelings were the following:

- I think I have the same, if not more, potential than those around me, but I don't get the results that they get.
- I know how to be fit but I choose not to follow through.
- I read books with the intent to learn from them but I don't follow the instructions for my own life.

It's okay to feel excited and it's okay to feel disappointed. Accepting feedback and having awareness are both stepping-stones towards making progress. It is what we do from here on out that is important. If we get stuck in either of these emotions, we can get trapped feeling over-confident or discouraged. Either will cripple our ability to perform at our full potential moving forward. Over-confidence can lead to losing the desire to improve and discouragement can lead to losing the desire to take action. So we must use those emotions to capture lessons that can fuel our best year ever!

Starting today, learn with the intent for short-term progress that will move you closer to the long-term goal. Eventually, you might get stuck and end up feeling guilty or anxious. Again, these are signs of awareness! This means you have a chance to improve and make the necessary adjustments. This is where a breakthrough happens and creates a lasting transformation in our lives.

To help gain some perspective on why this breakthrough is urgent and important, I want you to take a moment and think about how the average person lives their life. Think about how they handle relationships, how they approach their physical health, how they handle their emotions, and how they handle their finances. Take a moment and Google what the averages are in order to create some clarity about what your life will be like if you want to be *average*. Your search results will be something similar to this:

- ☐ 50% of marriages will end in divorce
- ☐ 69% of people are overweight or obese
- ☐ 80% of the population has some sort of debt
- ☐ 50% of people will have some mental disorder during their life

These stats are according to Centers for Disease Control and Prevention, American Psychological Association, and Fox Business News.

The average person approaches their life feeling as if they are incurable. They feel as if they are victims to circumstance and accept what happens to them, just like I did when I was in my early teens. Leaders and people who "GRAB" their futures are not willing to accept that. To someone who has control over his or her life, *incurable* could very well mean "curable from within". It's all a matter of perspective. Leaders take control and have a responsibility to perform – "response-ability" – the ability to respond.

The exciting benefit of the "Exercise to Thrive" is creating awareness of where you are, how you got there, where you are going, and what it will take to move forward. Leaders realize we choose our direction and make our desires happen. We choose not to allow anything to enter our mind that is not in alignment with our goals. We allow our inside voice to be louder than the voice of doubt. We train our thoughts by capturing them in writing and reading them daily. When we give ourselves permission to let our inside voice answer the questions "What does my 100% full potential look like? Am I living to that standard?", we will avoid the traps that the average person falls into.

The largest trap that people fall into is allowing limiting beliefs to influence their decision-making. What holds people back from being their best and creates their limiting beliefs are:

- Negative mindset
- Lack of confidence
- Unclear vision
- Lack of experience
- Fear
- Distractions

 Everyone experiences these, especially when challenges arise. It is a part of life and who we are. We can still stay in control and prevent them from getting in our way. In order to break through and perform at 100%, we must identify all our limitations from last year.

Exercise to Thrive Ten: Finding Your Limitations

We want to look back to last year and draw out all of the times where we didn't follow through, where we didn't walk the walk, where we felt bad for not reaching a goal we knew we could have met. We must remind ourselves of the disappointments as well, prior to moving forward.

For example: not following a morning routine, not investing time into my relationship with my sister, there's not enough time to get everything accomplished, accepting comfort after seeing results and not choosing to raise my standards to a new set of commitments.

What regrets/repeated mistakes were made last year? What limiting beliefs, behaviors, or patterns held me back from following through?

_____
_____
_____
_____
_____
_____
_____

_____

_____

_____

_____

_____

_____

_____

_____

_____

_____

_____

_____

The reason the average person continues to struggle is because they never change their patterns or their belief system, when these are holding them back. We can never do more than our current beliefs allow us to do.

The stories and excuses we tell ourselves when the results are low validate a very limiting belief that we are not capable of more; we then develop a pattern of not living up to our potential.

The definition of insanity is doing the same thing over and again and expecting different results. Therefore, a particular brand of insanity happens when you want to improve, but your detrimental beliefs remain unchanged. This leads to self-sabotage and creates mediocrity. Most of the causes for mediocrity are:

- Limiting beliefs
- Lack of urgency or a timeline
- Lack of self-discipline
- Insufficient personal development
- Lack of something to leverage

I think back to all the ways I self-sabotaged in my early teens. I knew what I wanted, but I kept getting in my own way. I kept believing my excuses and limiting myself to the reality of being overweight. Does the average person want this? Is this the plan or vision they see for themselves?

The average person often times settles into the "I tried it" mentality. They express personal concerns that they develop through their own experiences of failure, and then try to "protect" their loved ones from attempting what they couldn't do. They begin to experience the pain of watching others accomplishing goals that they knew they were capable of.

Is that what they truly want: to hold us back from our full potential?

You should no longer be willing to accept excuses for settling... for accepting mediocrity... for living up to less than your full potential. When challenges happen, we must ask ourselves better questions.

When everything feels like an Uphill struggle, just think of the view from the top

Instead of "Why me?", we can ask, "What were the barriers that held me back from taking action?" Better questions will allow you to unlock the tools you need to perform at peak level. Choose to ask better questions and you will change your life. This decision will create your destiny.

Creating your best year ever is about taking control and being responsible. It's not that the grass is naturally greener elsewhere, it's that we must actively become better gardeners. Someone once told me that if I am not the captain of my ship, then the ocean is.

Your best year ever is not about what you are doing, it is about who you are becoming. Are you learning? Growing? Listening? Contributing? Caring? Loving? If the entire world followed in your footsteps last year, would it be a better world?

Maybe we won't change the world, but we could change *someone's* world. Maybe you have a younger sibling or cousin looking up to you. Maybe a friend or an acquaintance is using your life as a map for theirs. Someone is looking up to us! As leaders, let's set our best year ever up in such a way as to make the world a better place for those we are inspiring.

By you taking the step to work through these exercises, you are already proving that you are capable of moving forward into "your best year ever". Now it's time to completely shift the paradigm and "flip the switch" on your life! I want you to think about what your mindset needs to be in order to reach your full potential. How must you view yourself? How must you view time? View challenges? View mornings? Think about the following phrase:

I must do _____ in order to become the person I need to be this year.

If we bring our beliefs from last year into this year, think about the dangers that could exist...? What could this cost you? How would it impact your health? Finances? Opportunities ahead? Imagine the unfilled potential! It would be a disaster for you to not exercise your full capacity! How important is it for you to break through these limiting factors? How important is it for you to re-write the story and GRAB your dreams?

Notes Page:

Chapter 3:
Creating Your Change NOW!

S.M.A.R.T. Strategies
"If I change, everything changes"

Let's recap:
>   We went through where we were last year.
>   We went through where we want to be beyond this year.

Now it's time to fill the gap and set S.M.A.R.T. goals for our best year
ever:

>   S - Specific
>   M - Measureable
>   A - Attainable
>   R - Realistic
>   T – Time frame

Specific – Have a precise target to shoot for. An easy way to create a
precise target is by answering a few simple questions:
>   ☐   *What do I want to get accomplished?*
>   ☐   *Where do I want it?*
>   ☐   *Who will be involved?*
>   ☐   *What will the time frame be?*
>   ☐   *Which things could get in my way?*
>   ☐   *Why do I want to this?*

Measurable – Have a way to measure your progress along the way
towards accomplishing your goals. You may have heard the saying
"results measured are results gained". An easy way to create this is by
answering these questions when setting your goals:
>   ☐   *How much?*
>   ☐   *How many?*
>   ☐   *How will I know when my goal is accomplished?*

Attainable – Have a mindset that you can achieve the goal, and a
goal that it is possible to achieve. Don't confuse an unattainable goal
for a simply ambitious one. If there are reasons as to why a goal is *not
within the realm of possibility*, don't use up valuable time and energy
on it.

Realistic – Have an objective that you are willing and able to work
towards. When measuring your own potential, you want to view
yourself not as who you are right now, but who you are when you're at
your best. Don't be afraid to reach high, but also make sure that

you're willing to give it your all.

Time Frame – Have a time frame that creates a sense of urgency. Without urgency, *someday* will never arrive. The time frame will put your subconscious mind into motion and urge you to make progress toward what you want to accomplish.

You are now finally ready to set your New Year's Resolutions and begin to live your best year ever! It's your time!

Exercise to Thrive Eleven: New Year's Resolutions

Looking back on all of the success and unattained results from last year, it is finally time to create the goals for "your best year ever"! It's time to think about what you want for this year, and also about the things you want to avoid. It's time to think about the person you want to be as you move towards your two-year goals and beyond. Keep in mind completing the unfinished goals from last year; it's not too late to make those your reality.

What do I want for this year? What do I want to avoid?

_____

_____

_____

_____

_____

_____

_____

_____

_____

_____

_____

_____

_____

_____

When I moved to college and started supporting myself, I had a desire to be completely independent from my parents. I wanted to earn my success without help. One of my mentors asked me, "Why do you want independence so badly that you're willing to go through such discomfort in your entrepreneurial efforts? Wouldn't it be easier for you to just ask for help?"

This question allowed me to gain clarity: I did indeed have a compelling reason, which fueled this motivation to take daily action steps towards my independence. I wanted control over my own outcomes because I wanted to create options for myself later in life. I feared getting *stuck* in life, you see. I feared needing to rely on others when I was older and when I chose to start a family. Having options and being in control motivated me.

Feeling trapped without control scared me, and avoiding the possibility of those fears coming true was the driving factor behind my daily action. I realized that I was more motivated by avoiding pain than creating pleasure. This was something I needed to learn about myself; I was now aware of the reasons and emotions that inspired me to be consistent in my efforts.

Now that you've figured out what you want and what you want to avoid, you must tie reasons to them. Reasons are what compel us to take action!

Exercise to Thrive Twelve: Reasons For New Year's Resolutions
Why do you want each of the goals you listed and why do you want to avoid the traps you thought about? By gaining clarity of your own reasons, you will make your goals REAL!

For example:
I want to <u>maintain at least a 3.8 G.P.A.</u> because <u>I want to earn a scholarship to fund college and not rely on my parents.</u>
I want to avoid <u>waking up after 8AM</u> because <u>I want to get more accomplished at the start of my day in order to feel more productive.</u>

I want _____ because? I want to avoid _____ because?

_____
_____
_____
_____
_____
_____

We now have a list of goals and traps to avoid, with reasons attached to each. This is so exciting! I am sure you are ready to take action towards living the life you deserve. It might be a little nerve-wracking because you have never done this before, thought this big before, or been this real with yourself before. Either way, I am excited for the person you are becoming through this process.

I think back to 2005 when I was twenty years old and I chose to keep my old 1991 Mitsubishi Eclipse and put my savings towards investing in my future. I decided to buy my first house! I had never studied real estate before and I just went out on a whim and bought a house. I rented out the rooms to other college students and had my rent covered. I was able to build credit and equity at a young age to kick start my experiences as an adult.

Today, I don't recommend this approach to investing in real estate; however, I do encourage taking action. Be sure to conduct some research about the housing markets, trends, and learn some principles about where to put your money before going out on a whim like I did.

But remember, I was eager to create a strong foundation for my future and to create options later on in my life. My vision of investing at a young age wasn't something that just popped into my head one day, staring at the sky. I read books and listened to mentors of mine who were very successful in their fields. I didn't really know where to put my money, but I knew I had to do something. So without much research, I chose to buy a house. I knew that if I wanted to create my best year ever, I couldn't do the same things the average person was doing. I had to be different... like I'm hoping you will be, as well.

Our final strategy in order to really make sure that our goals happen is to narrow them down to FIVE SPECIFIC outcomes. FIVE is the magic number. The idea is that, if you only accomplished FIVE of the goals on your list, you would still be grateful and see a dramatic change in your life.

Exercise to Thrive Thirteen: FIVE Specific Outcomes

From your list, what are FIVE SPECIFIC outcomes you want this year? I know it's challenging to pick just five, but narrow it down using your priorities in life.

My FIVE SPECIFIC outcomes are...

_____

_____

_____

_____

_____

_____

Now that you have your FIVE SPECIFIC outcomes, you are almost there! In order for the outcomes to become reality, we must be sure to have a routine in place that sets you up for success. We cannot allow ourselves to leave our goals in the hands of "wait and see" or "I will try". When emotions take over us, and they will, we must have a daily routine or pattern that is simple to follow and will create the habits needed to accomplish the goals we set.

Think about all of your daily routines that no longer take any thought: how you set your alarm, how you wash your body, how you brush your teeth, how you put your seatbelt on, how you open the car door, how you put on your shoes, etc. We stopped thinking at some point and those habits became a routine. When we eliminate the feelings and over-thinking, we create an environment of just *doing*! We must create that pattern!

Exercise to Thrive Fourteen: Daily Patterns Needed

For our final strategy, I want you to think about what pattern or daily routine must be in place in order to create daily momentum and progress towards EACH of your outcomes. You must understand that change is mandatory in order to make this your best year ever! It will be a good change, even though transition can be a little intimidating.

Example:

Goal – Strengthen relationship with my significant other

Potential Daily Actions – Give a gift, ask engaging questions, surprise visit at work, spontaneous trip, start a project together, create fun memories, take photos, share goals through a dream session.

What would need to happen DAILY in order for me to create progress towards EACH of my FIVE SPECIFIC outcomes?

_____

_____

_____

_____

_____

_____

_____

_____

_____

_____

_____

_____

_____

_____

Notes Page

Chapter 4:
Your Best Year Starts NOW!

FIVE Daily Actions
"Do or Do Not, There is No Try" – Yoda

Something I struggled with growing up and sometimes still do, is making decisions. It could be as small as what to order on the menu for dinner to bigger issues such as what college I wanted to attend. Sometimes my indecisiveness would cause me to miss out on important opportunities in my life. I remember in high school, wanting to ask a girl that I had a crush on out on a date. I really liked her and I wanted to make sure the timing was perfect. I had the whole scene mapped out in my head, but when I finally built up the courage to ask her out, she had already been taken! I missed out on ever having that chance; I still regret not taking immediate action.

This final step is to make it extremely simple to take action towards your goals daily. The outline is so simple it should be almost impossible to not achieve your goals! As long as something is simple for you to do daily, you'll do it! How do we both know that?

Because you made it to the end of this book! Often times, we will pick up a book and don't complete it. Your future self will be so proud of you and is looking forward to the life that you are about to create daily.

Exercise to Thrive Fifteen: Daily Actions List
Take your FIVE SPECIFIC outcomes and make a list of all of the actions that could be taken in order to make progress towards that goal. The longer the list of ideas, the more selective you can be later. You want to be specific with the list of actions. After completing each action, you MUST be able to look in the mirror and say, "I feel great! I made great progress today towards my goals of _____!" Be sure, then, to only add items to your list that will create this progress and emotion.

Example:

Specific Outcome: Lose 20 pounds
List of actions that could be taken:

- ☐ 100 crunches
- ☐ 50 jumping jacks
- ☐ 1 mile run in 10 min
- ☐ Eat a plant-based diet only
- ☐ Drink a ½ gallon of water with lemon
- ☐ Look up 5 healthy recipes for the week
- ☐ Attend a fitness class
- ☐ Foam roll exercises for 30 minutes
- ☐ Complete a hot yoga session
- ☐ Complete a 30-minute high intensity workout
- ☐ 5-mile bike ride

Specific Outcome #1: _____

Actions that could be taken to make progress towards that goal:

_____

_____

_____

_____

_____

_____

_____

_____

_____

_____

_____

_____

_____

_____

_____

_____

_____

_____

Specific Outcome #2: _____

Actions that could be taken to make progress towards that goal:

_____

_____

_____

_____

_____

_____

_____

_____

_____

_____

_____

_____

_____

_____

_____

Specific Outcome #3: _____

Actions that could be taken to make progress towards that goal:

_____

_____

_____

_____

_____

_____

_____

_____

_____

_____

_____

_____

_____

_____

_____

Specific Outcome #4: _____

Actions that could be taken to make progress towards that goal:

_____

_____

_____

_____

_____

_____

_____

_____

_____

_____

_____

_____

_____

Specific Outcome #5: _____

Actions that could be taken to make progress towards that goal:

_____

_____

_____

_____

_____

_____

_____

_____

_____

_____

_____

Once you have a list for each SPECIFIC outcome, you are now ready for the finale... "5 Things Daily!" This will ROCK your world and make you a productive machine! It is simple to follow and creates AMAZING progress towards your best year ever!

"5 Things Daily!" is a simple checklist that is made every night prior to going to bed. You pick one item from each list and write it in your planner for the next day. When you wake up, the first thing you want to do is look at the list and get to work! As you complete each task, check it off your list! At the end of the day, be prepared to feel OUTSTANDING! Then repeat the steps by making another list for the next day! "5 Things Daily!" will allow you to make small progress every day towards your dreams! Think about the end of the year, when you'll look at all of your accomplishments:

365 days x 5 things daily = 1,825 documented accomplishments!

Exercise to Thrive Sixteen: "5 Things Daily!"

1. Before bed tonight, pick one action from each Specific Outcome's list.
2. Write the list into your planner/calendar for tomorrow.
3. When you wake up, look at the list immediately.
4. As you complete each task, check it off the list.
5. Feel OUTSTANDING at the end of the day.
6. Repeat!!

The **JOURNEY** of a thousand miles begins with **ONE STEP.**

Conclusion
My Call To Action For You

Launching "your best year ever" is now within your grasp. You are the captain of your ship and the commander of your destiny. With all of the tools that you learned in this book, you are equipped to tackle every dream on your dreams list and have everlasting change for your life. I encourage you to re-read this book as often as you need to in order to maintain your drive and discipline.

There will be a moment in the near future when you do not "feel" like doing your "5 Things Daily" and work towards your specific outcomes. This is natural. The key is to "stay out of your head" and empty your thoughts daily into a journal. Science shows us that the physical act of writing down our thoughts can bring our emotions forward, control them, and not allow them to control us. So, included in your daily actions must be journaling through your thoughts. You might ask – "How do I journal? What do I write?" – which are the questions that I asked when I was first introduced to journaling. If you are like me in that regard, I would encourage you to use **G.R.A.B. Tomorrow: A Guided Journal to Capture Moments** to support you through the process. This is a great tool to ensure you are answering quality questions and giving yourself clarity on a consistent basis. You can order your copy online here: bit.ly/GRAByourThoughts

Your thoughts are one critical component of your "wheel of life" and must be managed, or else they will manage you. Other components include your health, relationships, time, money, passion, and legacy. If you're thinking the right way, but not treating your body the right way, you might not have the energy needed to fulfill your goals. This might begin to affect your relationships, finances, time, and the other parts of your "wheel". It's all connected and it's critical to be aware of when it's off-balance, so you can intentionally cultivate the strength and balance necessary to choose the direction you desire. This is often challenging due to the lack of resources, knowledge, or support that's needed on a consistent basis. To help you on your journey, I created the Simple 7 System™, which includes virtual workshops to guide you through each part of your "wheel of life" and ensure that you will have the tools to stay in control. You will be able conveniently use all of these workshops from any mobile device. Visit www.GRABtomorrow.org for more information on how to begin using the Simple 7 System™ today.

It's been an honor to provide these tools for you and I cannot wait to see the progress that comes from it. Leaders like you will create the desired changes in our communities.

The G.R.A.B. Community requires people who are no longer willing the accept average and are willing to take the steps to become OUTSTANDING! It is time to take control of your "tomorrow" and live the life you deserve! Go take it! It's Your Time!

Keep Me Posted On Your Journey: If you would like to share your progress, ask for feedback, or gain some resources from the G.R.A.B. Community, we would love to support you! Join the GRAB Community on Facebook! This group has great conversation topics that will inspire your daily decisions! www.facebook.com/groups/TheGRABcommunity

Blog: www.GRABtomorrow.org/apps/blog

YouTube: https://www.youtube.com/user/MikeASpeaks

Email: MikeAbramowitz@GRABtomorrow.org

www.GRABtomorrow.org

@MikeAbramowitz #GRABtomorrow

"Take control of life outside of the classroom."

Your "someday" is NOW and I am excited for you to go G.R.A.B. IT!
Go make an impact in your community!

Acknowledgments

Donald Abramowitz for stepping up and being both mom and dad when I needed you the most. For your ambition, drive, and care to make the world a better place.

Lindsay Fallon for your behind-the-scenes support daily, for your constant wisdom that compels me to improve, and for believing in me and my cause even when I waiver.

Matt King for your constant mentorship and guidance through the beginning stages of my vision and for encouraging me to keep my goals alive.

David Padron for supporting the first ever G.R.A.B. Tomorrow event and for being a great friend when I needed one.

Jane Hussar for inviting me into Countryside High School as a volunteer, community leader, and a friend; for inviting me to my first Great American Teach-in.

Joycee Patterson for being the first teacher to invite me into her classroom to speak to students about important life skills.

Kristin Clausen for supporting the G.R.A.B. philosophies and for finding a way to include them in your peer-to-peer mentoring program.

Amy Boylan for introducing me to the crazy world of middle school and for helping me find a passion for impacting those kids.

Stephanie Pawlowicz for believing in the G.R.A.B. program and incorporating it into your AVID program.

Chris Krimitsos for your time and wisdom in birthing the G.R.A.B. Tomorrow brand.

Eva Zoll for constantly pouring encouraging words and implementing, without fail, the G.R.A.B. concepts into your life.

JV Crum III for your wisdom and friendship, and for introducing me to amazing podcasters around the world.

Hal Elrod for leading the way as a person of influence, speaker, and expert in creating an online community and creating a vision from an idea.

Andrew Biggs for your coaching and guidance when it was needed most, to help me unlock my buried "lion" at the perfect time.

In Memoriam:

Eleanor Abramowitz for being the best mother I could have had, and for teaching me what it truly means to be strong.

Nick Shakes for showing me how to appreciate the life I have while creating the life of my dreams.

Next Action Steps

Implementation and accountability are critical in retaining the lessons you are learning. Here are a few tools to help you continue on your journey towards self-discovery and unlocking your full potential:

G.R.A.B. Tomorrow: Real Stories, Real People is filled with stories that are motivating, uplifting, sad, funny, and inspiring. Some stories will fill you with gratitude. Some stories will offer you perspective and lead you through paradigm shifts in how you approach your life. This #1 bestseller is featured in classroom programs to supplement the education process.

G.R.A.B. Your Thoughts: A Guided Journal To Capture Moments will help you maintain clarity and focus daily. By writing your responses to these impactful questions, you will avoid distractions and cultivate your own desire to make progress towards your goals.

G.R.A.B. Your Time: Weekly/Monthly Planner is designed to give you autonomy over the 168 hours in your week. It is paired with exercises and a video workshop to truly master time management.

G.R.A.B. Your Future: Simple 7 System™ is a 3-hour virtual workshop that will teach you how to control all facets of your wheel of life: Health, Thoughts, Relationships, Time, Money, Passion, and Legacy. Master these principles and you will enjoy true fulfillment.

G.R.A.B. Your Health: Elevated Fitness & Nutrition offers a plant-based alternative to your daily routine. Maintain your peak energy level by having the proper, delicious nutrition, and following some simple fitness guidelines.

G.R.A.B. Your Job Offers is a virtual workshop that will guide you through the DOs and DON'Ts of the interview process, but most importantly, it will show you how to prepare for this one-time opportunity to "sell yourself" to the hiring manager.

All of these tools are available online at:
www.GRABtomorrow.org/products-services

What is G.R.A.B. Tomorrow?

Grow, Re-evaluate, Appreciate, and Believe

G.R.A.B. Tomorrow started with the intent to help young professionals "take control of their lives outside of the classroom". Less than one year later, we launched a website (www.GRABtomorrow.org), a Facebook page that has since gathered two thousand supporters, a Facebook group with five hundred members, and the first book in the G.R.A.B. Tomorrow Series – "Your Best Year Ever" – was a #1 bestseller and has been purchased globally on four different continents. We began a local charity, "PB&J for Tampa Bay", where proceeds from book sales and other community support has helped provide over seven thousand meals during our first ten months.

The original goal of G.R.A.B. Tomorrow was to urge students and young professionals to follow their desires outside of the classroom, regardless of their circumstances or conditions, in order for them to thrive in a world where odds tend to be against them before they even enter it.

Even though the original focus was on helping these graduates, it has now turned into a community of people of all ages that choose to develop themselves, while making a difference in the areas that they live. All our members want to create options for themselves outside of a classroom. Along the way, the classroom's become something of a symbol – a metaphorical safe place from which we all need to graduate eventually. Stepping out of our comfort zones to enter the real world often involves dramatic change. There's no shame in needing to prepare yourself for those final steps, or in needing help to stand on your own two feet once you find yourself out there.

In order to share the impact of the G.R.A.B. Tomorrow philosophies, I decided to put together the series "Real Stories, Real People", so readers could see firsthand what "taking control of your life outside of the classroom" looks like. This series is filled with real-life situations that could happen to you or a loved one and will show you how members of the G.R.A.B. community chose to respond. This series is designed to inspire you to take control and build the life your potential offers you.

The original book in the series was released on December 20, 2015 and received #1 bestseller status in its first day. It went on to be a 3-time bestseller and is now being used as a part of the curriculum for AVID (Advancement via Individual Determination) students, along with other GRAB Tomorrow programs. In the near future, we will begin a podcast where the authors of these stories will be able to share their first hand experiences. As the series begins to expand, we will also have an annual event where the authors will take the stage to share their story and answer audience questions. We appreciate you joining us on this journey as we, together, continue to GRAB our Tomorrow and create the lives we desire.

Grow, Re-evaluate, Appreciate, and Believe – Your Someday is NOW: Capture it!

ABOUT THE AUTHOR

Mike Abramowitz is a District Executive for Vector Marketing and Cutco Cutlery, founder of PB&J for Tampa Bay, founder of The G.R.A.B. Community, and author of the #1 bestseller **G.R.A.B. Tomorrow: Real Stories, Real People.**

Despite starting his life as an overweight teen that lacked confidence and direction, and facing the adversity of losing his mother to a battle with cancer, Mike was able to prosper as a young entrepreneur. He was able to own three investment properties, operate a business to recruit and lead a sales team of students in his peer group that combined for $300,000 in sales over two summer breaks. He also managed a personal clientele of over five hundred that he created from scratch, and become an All-American Scholarship achiever. And all this before graduating college and his 23rd birthday.

Since earning his bachelors degree in industrial engineering with a minor in leadership studies from the University of South Florida in 2008, Mike has made a career in helping young professionals open their mindsets to what's possible when they fully commit to creating a strong foundation for their lives. He has trained and coached over four thousand young professionals to be entrepreneurs and sales representatives. He has interviewed over ten thousand applicants. As a keynote speaker, he has influenced over 20,000 audience members inside and outside of the classroom. He has been interviewed on several podcast radio shows, including Conscious Millionaire, Health Conscious Millionaire, MWF Motivation, I Am The One, Tropical Entrepreneur, and Turbo Charge Your Success.

Mike has a passion for providing tools, skills, and unlocking potential that's buried under socio-economic conditions and circumstances, lack of coaching, and fears that aspiring leaders face. He is a speaker, coach, author, and influences thousands of students each year through youth programs, assemblies, and in office training sessions.

To contact Mike about media appearances, speaking at your event or on campus, or if you just want to receive free training videos and resources, visit www.GRABtomorrow.org.

Mike resides in Clearwater, Florida and enjoys traveling, nature, sports, and guitar and has an addiction to self-help. He lives a plant-based lifestyle to keep healthy. He loves visiting his brother in Mexico and his dad and six other siblings in New Jersey.

34647727R00041

Made in the USA
Columbia, SC
30 November 2018